COMMUNITY · CONNECTIONS

GETTING TO KNOW OUR PLANET
FLORIDA WETLANDS

BY VICKY FRANCHINO

CHERRY
LAKE
Publishing

Published in the United States of America by Cherry Lake Publishing
Ann Arbor, Michigan
www.cherrylakepublishing.com

Content Adviser: Linda Hooper-Bùi, PhD, Associate Professor, Department of
Environmental Science, Louisiana State University Agricultural Center, Baton Rouge, Louisiana
Reading Adviser: Marla Conn, Read With Me Now

Photo Credits: Cover and page 1, © Svetlana Foote/Shutterstock.com; page 5,
© holbox/Shutterstock.com; page 7, © Kipling Brock/Shutterstock.com; page 9,
© Winthrop Brookhouse/Shutterstock.com; page 11, © Steve Bower/Shutterstock.com;
page 13, © mark higgins/Shutterstock.com; page 15, © FloridaStock/Shutterstock.com;
page 17, © Steven Blandin/Shutterstock.com; page 19, © Celso Diniz/Shutterstock.com;
page 21, © View Apart/Shutterstock.com.

LIBRARY OF CONGRESS CATALOGING-IN-PUBLICATION DATA
Names: Franchino, Vicky, author.
   Title: Florida wetlands / by Vicky Franchino.
Other titles: Community connections (Cherry Lake Publishing)
Description: Ann Arbor, Michigan : Cherry Lake Publishing, [2016] | 2014 |
   Series: Community connections | Series: Getting to know our planet |
   Audience: K to grade 3. | Includes bibliographical references and index.
Identifiers: LCCN 2015032431| ISBN 9781634705165 (lib. bdg.) |
   ISBN 9781634706360 (pbk.) | ISBN 9781634705769 (pdf) |
   ISBN 9781634706964 (ebook)
Subjects: LCSH: Wetland ecology—Florida—Everglades—Juvenile literature. |
   Everglades (Fla.)—Juvenile literature.
Classification: LCC QH104.5.S59 F73 2016 | DDC 577.6809759/39—dc23
LC record available at http://lccn.loc.gov/2015032431

Cherry Lake Publishing would like to acknowledge the
work of The Partnership for 21st Century Skills. Please
visit *www.p21.org* for more information.

Printed in the United States of America
Corporate Graphics
January 2016

FLORIDA WETLANDS

CONTENTS

A WATERY TREASURE

What do you imagine when you think of Florida? You might picture beaches and amusement parks. But there's also a natural treasure there. It's called the Florida Everglades. The Everglades is located at the southern tip of Florida. It covers 1.5 million acres (607,029 hectares). This area is an important **ecosystem**. It supports people, plants, and animals.

Parts of the Florida Everglades are wide stretches of long grass.

ASK QUESTIONS!

The Everglades is sometimes called a "river of grass." This is because of the tall, thick grasses there. What do you already know about the Florida Everglades? What would you like to learn more about?

5

The Everglades is a **wetlands** area. Water covers or soaks the soil most of the time. There are two types of wetlands. Coastal wetlands are near the ocean. The water in these areas is brackish. This means it is a mix of salt water and fresh water. Inland wetlands have only fresh water. You can find both kinds of wetlands in the Everglades.

The Everglades wetlands support a range of plants and animals.

The Everglades gets a lot of rain. About 5 feet (1.5 meters) falls each year. Most of it falls in the summer and fall. What happens when a lot of rain falls all at once? What problems occur?

SIX HABITATS

There are six **habitats** in the Everglades.

Hardwood **hammocks** are small islands covered with trees.

The pinelands are pine tree forests. Fires clear out other plants and give pines room to grow.

Mangrove **swamps** grow where rivers flow into the ocean. This meeting point is called an estuary.

Most trees need fresh water. But mangroves thrive in the brackish water of estuaries.

The roots of the mangrove tree are very unusual. They first arch above the ground. The rest of each root grows down into the soil. Look at the trees near where you live. Are there any that have unusual roots?

9

Saw grass **marshes** cover much of the Everglades. Watch out for the sharp edges of this grass. They can cut like a knife!

Cypress trees are right at home in cypress swamps. These trees grow well in very wet soil.

A slough is a flooded area that water travels through. The word slough rhymes with "moo." Sloughs usually feed into a larger body of water.

A bald cypress tree can grow to more than 150 feet (45 m) high.

The Florida Everglades became a national park in 1947. The Everglades is home to many different plants and animals. The park was created to protect these living things. Can you guess why this might be important?

11

WILDLIFE WONDERS

Only one place in the world has both alligators and crocodiles. That's the Everglades! Alligators like fresh water. Crocodiles live in salt water. The Everglades has both! How can you tell these two animals apart? Alligators have shorter, wider heads. Crocodiles are usually lighter in color.

A group of alligators hunts for dinner.

Alligators and crocodiles are cold-blooded. This means they can't control the temperature of their bodies. How might they cool off on a hot day? Or warm up when it's cold? Guess, and then check your answer. Were you right?

Hundreds of types of birds are found in the Everglades. Some live there. Others stop by during **migration**. Why do birds like the Everglades? The temperatures are warm. Also, birds can easily find materials to build a nest. There's plenty to eat as well. Egrets, herons, and wood storks live in the Everglades. Whooping cranes and falcons travel through as they migrate north or south.

Purple gallinules live in the Everglades all year long.

THINK!

The Everglades was once twice the size it is today. People drained the wetlands to build homes, roads, and farms. What are some good things that happened because of this? What problems do you think these actions might have caused?

15

The Everglades has had many changes over the years. These have put dozens of animals in danger of dying out. Many of the birds that once lived there are now gone. Today, the Florida panther is the region's most **endangered** animal. The manatee lives in the water. It looks a bit like a seal. It is endangered, too.

Fewer than 100 Florida panthers live in the wild today.

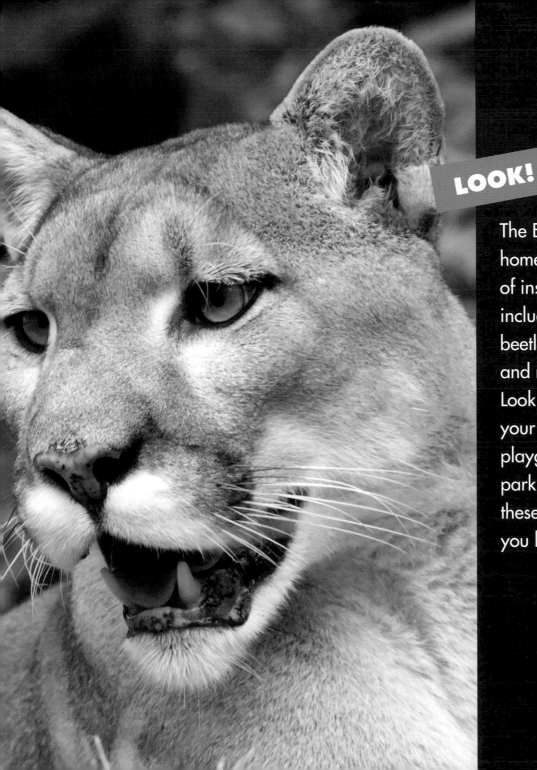

LOOK!

The Everglades is home to many kinds of insects. These include whirligig beetles, dragonflies, and mosquitoes. Look carefully around your yard, the school playground, or a park. Do you have these insects where you live?

17

PEOPLE OF THE EVERGLADES

Native people have lived in the Everglades for hundreds of years. Then European settlers first arrived in the 1500s. These people thought the swamp areas were worthless. Later, people drained the swamp. They built houses, roads, and farms on the dried land. These changes damaged the land.

Engineers started taking water out of the Everglades in the 1800s. They used it to supply nearby cities such as Miami, Florida.

Some Native Americans still live in the Everglades. Many of them live in traditional homes of wood and leaves. Others have more modern dwellings. Think about what is good about each type of home. What is bad? Which would you choose?

19

Today, people know how important the Everglades is. One of its most important jobs is to store and **filter** water. This provides clean water to plants, animals, and people. Many groups work hard to protect the land. They hope to preserve the Everglades for years to come.

The Florida Everglades is a beautiful place. Would you like to visit it?

Programs at Everglades National Park help people learn more about the region.

What do you find most interesting about the Everglades? Create a piece of art about something you learned. You could make a drawing or write a poem. You can even make up a song! The choice is up to you!

GLOSSARY

ecosystem (EE-koh-sis-tuhm) the living things in a place and their relationship to their environment

endangered (en-DAYN-jurd) at risk of dying out completely

filter (FIL-tur) to clean liquids, such as water, as they move through a place

habitats (HAB-i-tats) places where a plant or animal is usually found

hammocks (HAM-uhks) groups of hardwood trees growing on a raised area that is surrounded by wetlands

marshes (MAHRSH-iz) areas of wet, muddy land

migration (mye-GRAY-shun) the act of moving to another area or climate at a specific time of year

swamps (SWAHMPS) areas of wet, spongy ground

wetlands (WET-landz) areas where there is a lot of moisture in the soil

FIND OUT MORE

BOOKS

Furstinger, Nancy. *The Everglades: The Largest Marsh in the United States*. New York: AV2 by Weigl, 2014.

Larsen, Laurel. *One Night in the Everglades*. New York: Moonlight Publishing, 2012.

WEB SITES

Everglades Foundation: Quick Facts
www.evergladesfoundation.org/the-everglades/facts
Learn some fun facts about the Everglades.

National Geographic: Everglades National Park
http://travel.nationalgeographic.com/travel/national-parks /everglades-national-park
Everglades National Park is a national treasure. Learn more about it here!

INDEX

24

ABOUT THE AUTHOR

Vicky Franchino loves to learn about new places and (usually!) wants to visit each one of them. She thinks it would be very exciting to visit the Florida Everglades—although if she saw an alligator or crocodile, she would like it to be far, far away! Vicky lives in Wisconsin with her family, a place where alligators and crocodiles are only at the zoo.